STUDENT'S ACTIVITY BOOK for

Journey Through Jewish History

The Age of Faith and The Age of Freedom

Morris J. Sugarman

Behrman House, Inc.

To the memory of my grandmother
Ethel Leah Silverman-
the wise and loving matriarch of our family.

ISBN: 0-87441-376-1

Illustrations by Richard Rosenblum

Book design by Marsha Picker

Contents

Who Were They?*

In the left-hand column you see a list of people important in Jewish history. In the right-hand column is a list of definitions. Write the number of each person next to the proper description.

People

1. Moses

2. Saul and David

3. Gideon, Samson, and Deborah

4. The Romans

5. Cyrus the Great

6. The Prophets

7. Nebuchadnezzar

8. Hillel, Akiba, Meir, and Rabbi Judah the Prince

9. The Geonim

Descriptions

___ Judges

___ Made the first collection of Oral Law which became Mishnah

___ Led the children of Israel to Mount Sinai, where a Covenant was made between them and God for all time.

___ Israel's first kings

___ The king whose armies destroyed the Temple in Jerusalem in 586 B.C.E.

___ Believed that they had put an end to the Jewish people when they destroyed the Second Temple in 70 C.E.

___ The Persian king who allowed the Jews to return to Jerusalem

___ The heads of the schools of Babylonia

___ Taught that God loved kindness and justice more than Temple sacrifices

* Answers to all starred exercises are in the Answer Key at the end of the activity book.

Turning Points

A turning point in history is a major event that gives shape and direction to the future. The covenant between God and Abraham and Sarah is one such turning point. And there are a number of others that you read about in your textbook. Jewish history has been described as a climb up a mountain. The path on the "mountainside" below begins with the covenant, and stops at the First Council of Nicaea, which decided that Christianity should break away from its Jewish past completely — a major event that paved the way for the persecution of Jews in the Middle Ages. What were the important turning points between these two events? Write them in the order in which they happened on the mountain path.

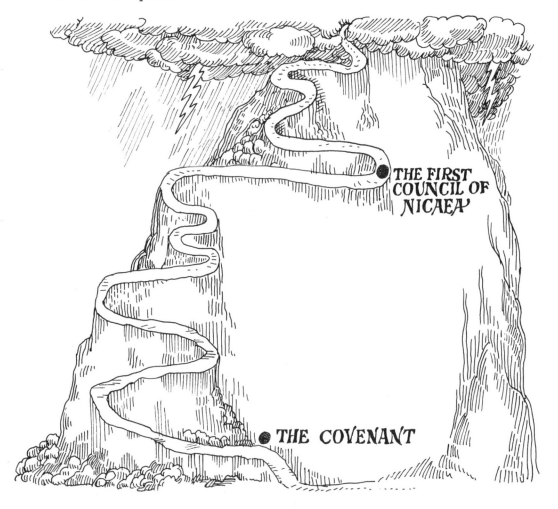

Secrets Of Survival*

Hidden in the letters below are seven words that have helped the Jewish people survive. Look across and down to find the hidden words and then circle them.

```
C  S  P  R  A  Y  E  R  B  C
O  F  Y  X  Z  T  M  F  C  O
M  G  U  N  T  O  R  A  H  V
M  I  W  V  A  X  S  I  K  E
U  T  D  H  L  G  L  T  J  N
N  M  S  Y  M  I  O  H  N  A
I  Z  F  T  U  N  R  G  Z  N
T  S  T  U  D  Y  Q  T  U  T
Y  M  O  J  H  N  Y  O  G  E
```

_____   _____

_____   _____

_____   _____

_____

Who, What, and Where Am I?*

1. I am a city that became the center of Christianity in the Middle Ages.

_____

2. I am the emperor who made Christianity the equal of all other religions in the Roman Empire.

_____

3. I am the pope who labeled the Jewish people the worst enemy of Christianity, but at the same time, offered money to any Jews who would convert.

_____

4. I am the area, which today spans France and Germany, from which European Jewry took its name.

_____

5. I am the scholar and teacher who wrote commentaries explaining the Bible and Talmud.

_____

6. I am a "soldier" who marched to conquer the Holy Land in the name of Christianity, and looted, destroyed, and murdered Jews.

_____

7. I am the idea that it is sometimes better for Jews to choose death, rather than to give up their religion. My English translation is "Sanctification of the Name (of God)."

_____

8. I am the rabbi who persuaded my community to choose Sanctification of the Name of God, and to offer up our lives rather than be captured by an army of English "soldiers of Christianity."

_____

Be Rashi

Rashi, and the tosafists who followed him, deeply believed that the Bible and Talmud were not the private property of scholars. They belonged to all the Jewish people. So they took it upon themselves to teach, to comment, and to explain, so that we might better understand and make these ideas a part of our lives.

Imagine that you are Rashi and explain the meaning of the story on page 24 to your "students." Their notion of fine merchandise may be a color T.V. set, a video game, or a home computer. In the space below write how you would help them understand the idea of "the best merchandise . . . called Torah."

_____

_____

_____

_____

_____

_____

Notes From A Traveler's Diary

A traveler, touring the Jewish communities of Ashkenaz during the Middle Ages, could have written the following statements in his diary. Can you support each of these impressions with a reference to, or a direct quotation from, your textbook? Be sure to look carefully at the illustrations too.

1. They have a strong sense of responsibility for one another.

_____

_____

2. They have a deep relationship to their biblical past.

_____

_____

3. They live in their own separate world, but they manage to be part of the non-Jewish world, as well.

_____

_____

4. They value the study of the Torah.

_____

_____

Define the Terms

You have read about each of these words in your textbook. What does each word mean?

1. The "Host"

_____

_____

2. Disputations

_____

_____

3. Black Death

_____

_____

4. Blood Libel

_____

_____

5. "The Light of the Exile"

_____

_____

6. The Tosafists

_____

_____

7. Yeshivot

_____

_____

Read All About It!*

The following headlines could have been written by Christian journalists during the Middle Ages. Of course, their view of things would be quite different from ours, but on the basis of the content of each headline, see if you can identify the event.

Medieval Times

LAST KNIGHTS
JOUSTING
FINALS

1. **CHILD MURDER MYSTERY SOLVED**

   _____

2. **BONFIRES BRIGHTEN PARIS SKIES**

   _____

3. **RABBI REFUSES TO PAY PRICE OF FREEDOM**

   _____

4. **AUTHORITIES UNCOVER CAUSE OF DREAD DISEASE**

   _____

5. **NEW JEWISH CLOTHING STYLES ORDERED**

   _____

6. **DEBATER DRIVEN OUT OF COUNTRY**

   _____

Statements To Think About

Choose any one of the statements below, and in your own words, tell how the material in the chapter shows it to be true.

1. Prejudice's natural allies are ignorance and superstition.

2. Repeat a lie often enough, and people begin to believe that it's true.

3. When things go bad, people look for someone to blame.

4. Very often, the question is not *"Who is right and who is wrong?"* but rather, *"Who has the power?"*

_____

_____

_____

_____

_____

_____

_____

_____

_____

_____

_____

Words and Meanings*

Match each word in the left column with its correct definition in the right column. Place the number of each word in the space before its meaning.

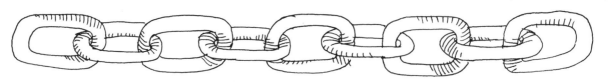

Word	*Definition*
1. Mysticism	____ The basic textbook for Jewish mystics
2. The Kabbalah	____ The countless levels of knowing God
3. Hasid	____ The individual, sent by God, who would redeem the Jewish People, and lead them to the Land of Israel at the End of Days, ushering a time of peace and love forever
4. The Zohar	
5. The Messiah	
6. Sefirot	____ A very pious individual
	____ The process of trying to enter the world of God
	____ The long chain of Jewish mystical teachings—called "tradition" in English

The Reasons Why

1. A number of false Messiahs appeared in the Middle Ages because

_____

_____

2. Moses de Leon claimed that the Zohar was not written by him, but by Rabbi Simeon bar Yohai because

_____

_____

3. The Talmud warned that a person should not study mysticism until the age of forty because

_____

_____

4. The *Bahir* compares the world of the spirit to an onion because

_____

_____

5. The idea of the Messiah has always been an important part of Judaism because

_____

_____

The End of Days

The End of Days will usher in a messianic era—a time when the world will be peaceful and free of suffering. There have been many different ideas of what the End of Days will be like. What are yours? In the space below, write, in specific terms, your version of the End of Days.

_____

_____

_____

_____

Since the Messiah has not yet come, how would you make the world a better place today? Imagine that you have been granted a single wish to help improve things. What would that wish be—and why?

_____

_____

_____

_____

Who, What, and Where Am I?*

1. I am the "government" which supervised the communal, educational, political, and religious affairs of Jews in Poland and Lithuania.

   _____

2. I am the invention that revolutionized intellectual life in Europe, and gave Jews the opportunity to have copies of their holy books.

   _____

3. I am the name that was given to walled-in Jewish neighborhoods in European cities.

   _____

4. I am the book that contains the code of Jewish laws—a guidebook for Jews throughout the world.

   _____

5. I am the author of the above book.

   _____

6. I am the name given to Jewish communities that were set up in small country villages in Eastern Europe.

   _____

7. I am the word used to describe the tradition of Jews lending a helping hand to other Jews.

   _____

8. I am an Italian Jewish Renaissance thinker who tried to analyze Jewish history, law, and legend in a modern way.

   _____

9. I am the author of *Ha-Mappah* (the "Tablecloth"), the collection of Ashkenazi customs, which was added to the original code of Jewish laws.

   _____

In Addition

You have read about the following terms in your textbook. Add one more fact to each.

1. The Ghetto
   a. could be found in all the major cities in Europe.
   b. derived its name from the word "foundry."
In addition,

---

2. The Shtetl
   a. was located in the countryside and could be called a ghetto without walls.
   b. was often protected by the government.
In addition,

---

3. The Renaissance
   a. was a period of great intellectual and cultural activity.
   b. freed Christian thinkers from the intellectual restrictions imposed by the church.
In addition,

---

4. The Shulhan Aruch
   a. is a guidebook of Jewish laws.
   b. contains the customs of both Ashkenazi and Sephardi Jewry.
In addition,

---

5. The Christians
   a. forbade the Jews to enter certain occupations.
   b. levied very heavy taxes upon the Jewish communities.
In addition,

Traveling Through Time

The Jewish way of life has been described—at the very beginning of the textbook—as "a great journey through time and place." Imagine that a Jewish boy and girl from a sixteenth century ghetto have managed to "travel" to the present. What would you point out to them as the greatest differences between Jewish life in the ghetto and Jewish life in your own community today? Are there any similarities?

_____

_____

_____

_____

_____

_____

Cause and Consequence

Complete each of the following causes with one important consequence that it brought about.

1. Because the Jews refused to accept Muhammad as a prophet,

_____

_____

2. Because Muhammad told the story of resting in Jerusalem before rising to "the seventh heaven,"

_____

_____

3. Because Mecca had a good supply of water,

_____

_____

4. Because Muhammad met many Jews and Christians in his travels,

_____

_____

5. Because the Jews and Christians worshiped the One God,

_____

_____

6. Because Muhammad had a powerful personality,

_____

_____

The Five Pillars of Islam*

Unscramble each of the word groups to reveal an idea that expresses one of the *Pillars* of Islam. Write the unscrambled idea inside its pillar.

1. GOD IS BUT ALLAH ONE NAME THERE AND IS HIS

2. SINGLE GOD EVERY A PRAY MUSLIM TO MUST DAY

3. WAY FASTING A IS GOD TO PRAYING OF

4. HELPING PEOPLE IN A LEND TO HAND THE MIDST YOUR POOR

5. PILGRIMAGE HOLY ISLAM THE OF PLACES A MAKE TO

A Merchant's Journal*

A merchant traveling the trade routes during the seventh and eighth centuries, visited many interesting places. And if he had kept a journal of his travels, it might have contained entries like the ones below. Can you name each place described? Refer to the printed material in the chapter as well as the illustrations and the map.

1. What a relief to finally get here, after all those hours in the desert. A real oasis. . . and a holy city, too, from what I hear.

2. This body of water is a trader's dream. Egypt to my left, Yemen to the east, and soon the southern tip of Palestine.

3. I wouldn't have believed it! A Jewish community right in the middle of the desert! And a Christian community just south of here! Maybe this country is going to become the new center of monotheism—a religious showplace dedicated to the worship of the One God!

4. What a magnificent structure. It stands where the ancient Jewish Temple once stood. People believe that this is the spot where Abraham came to sacrifice Isaac.

5. I must have met traders here from more than a dozen countries. This great city of Israel's large northern neighbor is so big and sprawling. I wonder how the people must have felt when their armies were defeated by the Maccabees.

6. Back again in the City of David, with its majestic hills and golden sunlight on its stone buildings. No wonder it is considered a holy city by all three religions.

How Do You Know?

Find a fact in the chapter to prove each statement. Be sure to examine the photographs and the illustrations too.

1. There was active contact between Jewish communities in different countries during this period.

_____

_____

_____

2. Spanish Jews lived in two worlds—Jewish and Muslim—at the same time, and were able to strike a successful balance between the two cultures.

_____

_____

_____

3. The Jews of Spain not only observed the traditions of Judaism, they added to them as well.

_____

_____

_____

4. The Spanish Jewish community valued scholarship and learning.

_____

_____

_____

Notable Achievements*

Read the descriptions on each award, and then write the name of the person to whom it could be awarded.

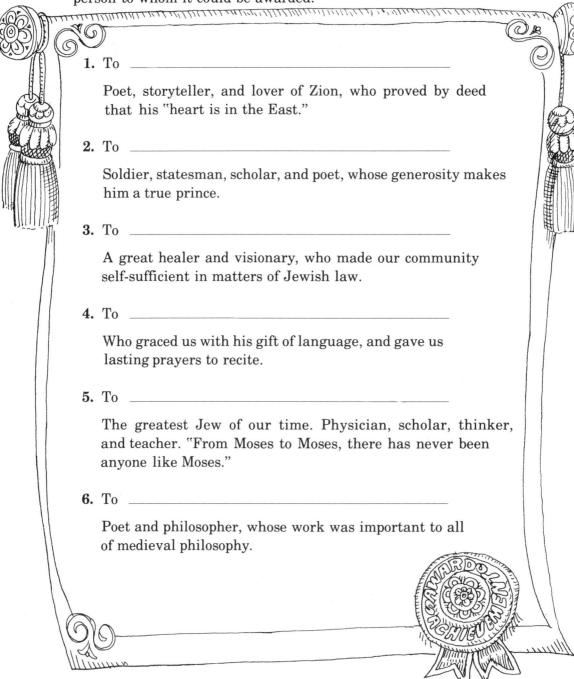

1. To _____

Poet, storyteller, and lover of Zion, who proved by deed that his "heart is in the East."

2. To _____

Soldier, statesman, scholar, and poet, whose generosity makes him a true prince.

3. To _____

A great healer and visionary, who made our community self-sufficient in matters of Jewish law.

4. To _____

Who graced us with his gift of language, and gave us lasting prayers to recite.

5. To _____

The greatest Jew of our time. Physician, scholar, thinker, and teacher. "From Moses to Moses, there has never been anyone like Moses."

6. To _____

Poet and philosopher, whose work was important to all of medieval philosophy.

Book Reviews*

The "Golden Age" of Spain witnessed the flowering of a magnificent Jewish culture. Many great books were written during this period. Read each of the reviews below, and then write in the name of the book that it is discussing, and the name of the author.

1. This work proves that Jewish and Muslim ideas do not contradict one another. They can coexist.

_____

2. A dramatic and original way to get across the meaning and message of the Jewish faith, while giving a clear view of Christianity and Islam as well.

_____

3. Prayers, like anything else, need order—and the fact that they have now been written down gives us a sense of their permanence.

_____

4. This book makes the point that Judaism is not just a religion of the mind; kindness and compassion are as important as scholarship.

_____

5. What this book does is simplify a very complicated subject—Talmud—and make it possible for more and more people to learn and understand our laws.

_____

Your Two "Selves"

Like our ancestors in the "Golden Age" of Spain, we too, as American Jews, move back and forth between two cultures. Each has its distinctive set of aims, values, and demands. Take a thoughtful look at your American "self" and your Jewish "self" and answer the following questions.

1. Which elements of your day-to-day life are expressions of your American "self?"

_____

_____

_____

2. Which elements of your day-to-day life are expressions of your Jewish "self?"

_____

_____

_____

3. Are there any ways in which your American "self" hinders your Jewish "self" from full expression?

_____

_____

_____

4. Are there any ways in which your being an American helps make you a better Jew?

_____

_____

_____

In Addition

Add one more fact or idea to each of the statements below. Make your choice, in each case, on the basis of what you think is most important.

1. The Inquisition
    a. was a committee of churchmen charged with the task of making Spain a completely Christian country.
    b. was headed, from 1484 on, by Tomas de Torquemada.

In addition,

_____

_____

2. The Marranos
    a. derived their name from the Spanish word for "swine."
    b. lived in a state of continuing danger, for discovery usually meant torture or death.

In addition,

_____

_____

3. Ferdinand and Isabella
    a. were sometimes called the "Catholic kings."
    b. conquered the last Muslim province and united Spain.

In addition,

_____

_____

4. The New World
    a. was invaded by Spanish and Portuguese conquistadores searching for gold.
    b. was not free of the Inquisition.

In addition,

_____

_____

Who, What, When, and Where Am I?*

1. I am the year in which the Jews were officially driven out of Spain.

_____

2. I am the city in which the first Jewish community in the New World was established.

_____

3. I am the last Muslim province to be conquered by Christian Spain—with frightening consequences for the Jewish community.

_____

4. I am the name given to Jews who chose to practice their Judaism secretly.

_____

5. I am the place where the first Jews settled in North America, in 1654.

_____

6. I am the name given to Spanish and Portuguese soldiers of fortune, who came to the New World in search of riches.

_____

7. I am the religious leader who conducted a merciless campaign, murdering unfaithful Christians and secret Jews.

_____

The Ingredients of the Inquisition*

The Spanish Inquisition did not just happen. It was the result of a number of crucial ingredients. All of the ingredients below, with the exception of one, contributed to the Inquisition. Circle the number before the ingredient that would have made the Inquisition unlikely, and explain why.

1. The belief that your religion is the only true religion.
2. The belief that everyone should worship your way.
3. A population that fears and obeys.
4. A democratic government elected by all the people.
5. The belief that persecution, torture, and murder, done in the name of religion, are morally acceptable means.

Reason

_____

_____

_____

_____

On The Move*

During the sixteenth and seventeenth centuries, the Jews of Spain and Portugal were a people on the move—desperately seeking places of refuge from the Inquisition. Families, friends, and neighbors were forced to separate, and communication between them was severely limited. The following letters might have been written by Jews moving from one place to another during those anxious times. Using the text and the map on page 62 as your references, try to figure out from where each of these letters was sent.

1. I am right in the middle of the Inquisition, but from this city I can book passage to the New World.

2. We worked our way across the Mediterranean on a merchant ship from Palermo—and are thinking of settling in this lovely port city in the "Land of the Pharaohs."

3. We've seen the River Thames. I am still worried—considering our past history here—but at least this is now a Protestant country.

4. We came up from Naples. But as for settling here permanently, it is too close to the Vatican.

5. The Jewish community here continues to grow—thanks to the effort of our "Angel." We find safety in a city named after a ruler who put Christianity on the map. Do you know that the Jews in this country have created their own special language?

6. Here we are in a city that granted its Jews freedom of religion, and the Jews refuse freedom of thought and expression to one of our own people.

In The Headlines*

Each of the following newspaper headlines refers to an event you read about in your textbook. Can you identify the event?

SEPHARDI TIMES

1. **A RETURN AFTER 300 YEAR ABSENCE**

   _____

   _____

2. **A PERSON WITHOUT A PEOPLE**

   _____

   _____

3. **PLAN TO POPULATE HOLY LAND FAILS**

   _____

   _____

4. **RANSOMED AFTER 2 YEAR IMPRISONMENT**

   _____

   _____

The Reasons Why

1. The Jews of Holland excommunicated Spinoza because

_____

_____

_____

2. Dona Gracia Mendez Nasi was called the "Angel of the Marranos" because

_____

_____

_____

3. The Jews were allowed to practice their religion in Holland freely and openly because

_____

_____

_____

4. The Jewish language called Ladino (the Sephardic version of Yiddish) came into being because

_____

_____

_____

5. England permitted Jews to live there after an absence of 300 years because

_____

_____

_____

Words And Meanings*

Match the word in the left column with its proper meaning in the right column. Make your choice by placing the number of the word in the space before its meaning.

1. Pilpul

2. Kavvanah
   (or Devekut)

3. Tsaddik

4. Tikkun

5. Maggid

6. Mitnagged

_____ A very righteous individual. The name given to many Hasidic leaders.

_____ A Hasidic teller of stories and fables.

_____ An individual—usually a religious scholar—who strongly opposed Hasidism.

_____ The literal translation of this word is "pepper." It is the practice of concentrating upon small, obscure points of law, that have little relevance to the lives of most Jews.

_____ The literal translation of this word is "repair." A mystical idea which teaches that through continuing devotion, we can make God's light rise again to the heavens, and bring the days of the Messiah ever closer.

_____ A deep and passionate devotion to God. Clinging to God "with all your heart, with all your soul, and with all your might."

A Leader's Speech*

Each of the speeches below might have been made by one of the individuals discussed in the chapter. All of them—good and evil—were remarkable leaders. Identify the leader on the basis of each speech's content.

1. We have just come through the darkest of times. What better proof do we need that the End of Days is at hand? As our prophet Moses led his people from their country of bondage to the Promised Land, so I shall one day lead you. Believe in my words! Believe in me!

2. Reject these magicians, these miracle-workers, these dancing, storytellers! They take you away from true Judaism—from the study of the Torah and Talmud.

3. Rise up with me! Throw-off the yoke of the oppressors. Let's talk to these princes and noblemen and rich landowners in the only tongue that they understand: the language of the sword!

4. If you study and pray with all of your being, the world will glow with the light of the Lord, and all of humankind.

5. Of course the Torah and Talmud are important, but they are not the only things that are holy. Life is holy. People are holy. Nature is holy. And God can be found everywhere—in the rustle of a tree, in a melody, in the movement of a dance.

Cause And Consequence

Complete each of the following causes with one important consequence that it brought about.

1. Because of the Chmielnicki massacres,

_____

_____

_____

2. Because Shabbetai Zevi proclaimed that he was the Messiah,

_____

_____

_____

3. Because the Jews in Eastern Europe were taxed to the point of poverty,

_____

_____

_____

4. Because fewer and fewer Jews were able to study the Torah and Talmud properly,

_____

_____

_____

5. Because Hasidism became so popular,

_____

_____

_____

In Addition

Add one more fact to each of the statements below. Make your addition on the basis of what you think is most important.

1. Moses Mendelssohn
   a. was permitted to leave the ghetto and study in Berlin.
   b. always remained an Orthodox Jew.
In addition,

2. Court Jews
   a. were often among the brightest or richest Jews of their time.
   b. often dressed and spoke the language of their non-Jewish neighbors.
In addition,

3. The Jews of Mendelssohn's time
   a. lived a life apart from their Christian neighbors.
   b. were not allowed to work at most jobs.
In addition,

4. The Age of Reason
   a. opened the door to many new and exciting ideas.
   b. brought about a revolution in human rights.
In addition,

Visions And Values*

Unscramble the word groups below to discover Mendelssohn's most cherished visions and values.

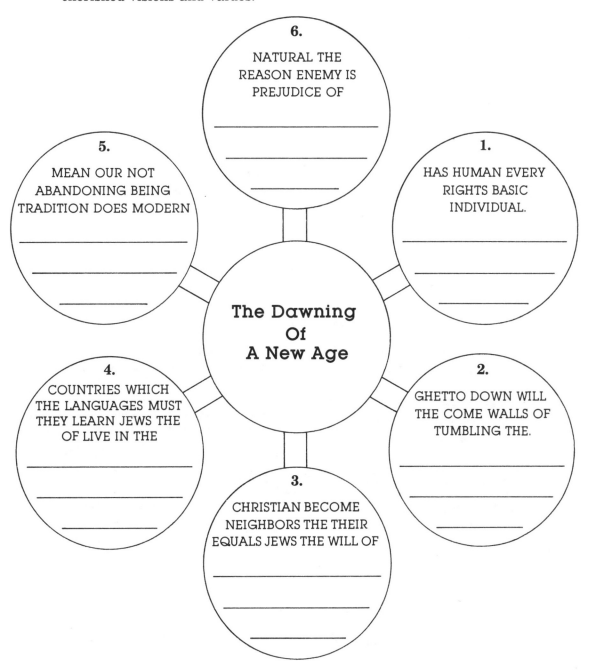

6.
NATURAL THE REASON ENEMY IS PREJUDICE OF
_____
_____
_____

5.
MEAN OUR NOT ABANDONING BEING TRADITION DOES MODERN
_____
_____
_____

1.
HAS HUMAN EVERY RIGHTS BASIC INDIVIDUAL.
_____
_____
_____

The Dawning Of A New Age

4.
COUNTRIES WHICH THE LANGUAGES MUST THEY LEARN JEWS THE OF LIVE IN THE
_____
_____
_____

2.
GHETTO DOWN WILL THE COME WALLS OF TUMBLING THE.
_____
_____
_____

3.
CHRISTIAN BECOME NEIGHBORS THE THEIR EQUALS JEWS THE WILL OF
_____
_____
_____

Looking For Understanding

Answer the following questions briefly and clearly.

1. What, exactly, was a shtadlan, and why was he a key figure in the Jewish community?

_____

_____

_____

_____

2. How would you define the Age of Reason—and why did Mendelssohn believe that it would also be a time of hope and opportunity for the Jewish people?

_____

_____

_____

_____

3. On the basis of what you have read in the chapter, describe the kind of life that Mendelssohn had in mind for future generations of Jews.

_____

_____

_____

_____

4. Why do you think that the new freedom proved to be so dangerous for our people?

_____

_____

_____

_____

Find The Outsider*

In each of the statements below, circle the letter before the section that is untrue.

1. Leopold Zunz   (**a**) wanted his people to be proud of being Jews   (**b**) tried to show that Judaism was constantly developing and could meet the challenges of modern life   (**c**) used methods of scientific scholarship to study Jewish texts   (**d**) believed that Judaism was out of step with modern times.

2. Heinrich Heine   (**a**) converted for practical, rather than religious, reasons   (**b**) would never have become a poet if he had not converted   (**c**) found himself an outsider in both the Jewish and Christian worlds   (**d**) never stopped thinking of himself as a Jew.

3. Napoleon   (**a**) granted citizenship to the Jews because he wanted their money and influence   (**b**) wanted the Jews to be loyal citizens of France   (**c**) freed the Jews in every country that he conquered   (**d**) called Jewish leaders together in a Sanhedrin.

4. The Enlightenment   (**a**) inspired the French Revolution   (**b**) brought new ideas of equality   (**c**) fought against all religions (**d**) led to the emancipation of the Jews.

5. Emancipation   (**a**) made the Jews equal citizens under the law   (**b**) allowed the Jews to leave their ghettos   (**c**) gave the Jews opportunities they had never known before   (**d**) brought an end to all prejudice and anti-Semitism   (**e**) caused a number of Jews to move away from their traditional way of life.

And Yet. . .

History rarely moves in a straight line. It zigzags and backslides, and progress is usually punctuated with a series of "And yet's."

The story of Jewish emancipation in Europe is marked by a number of "And yet's." Try your hand at completing the following statements.

1. Heinrich Heine's conversion opened doors for him in Christian society. And yet,

_____

_____

_____

2. When they were in the ghetto, the Jews cherished and valued their way of life. And yet,

_____

_____

_____

3. With emancipation, the Jews were considered legally equal to their Christian neighbors. And yet,

_____

_____

_____

4. Now that they were free and enjoyed civil rights, Jews could practice their religion more easily and openly than ever before. And yet,

_____

_____

_____

Hopes For The Future*

Each of the scrambled words below was a hope of the Jews of Europe after their emancipation. Unscramble them. Place them in the boxes that follow. Then, unscramble the circled letters to reveal a development that cast an unhappy shadow on this new era.

1. MODREEF

2. SECTYRUI

3. EQITYLUA

4. ROUTOPPTINY

5. TEPANCCEAC

6. EDTIONUCA

Biographical Dictionary

Write what you have learned about each of the following people.

Peter Stuyvesant

_____

_____

_____

Roger Williams

_____

_____

_____

Asser Levy

_____

_____

_____

Aaron Lopez

_____

_____

_____

Haym Salomon

_____

_____

_____

What We Can Learn*

In each of the statements below, circle the letter before the lesson that cannot be drawn from the material in the chapter.

1. From the section AMERICAN VALUES, JEWISH VALUES, we learn that
   a. many important American values were learned from the Bible.
   b. the Jews were granted full rights of citizenship by the Constitution.
   c. American Jews made it their business to read the works of Mendelssohn.

2. From the maps and photographs, we learn that
   a. Jews settled in towns and cities near the coast.
   b. the Jews built their synagogues on a small, modest scale, in order not to offend the Christians.
   c. there have been synagogues in this country for well over 300 years.

3. From the section dealing with Jews in the Revolution, we learn that
   a. the fact that some Jews remained loyal to Great Britain sparked a good deal of anti-Semitism among Christian Americans.
   b. there were Jews who made enormous sacrifices on behalf of the Revolution.
   c. the ideas contained in the Declaration of Independence were a source of hope for many Jews.

4. From the material dealing with the settlement of Jews in the colonies, we learn that
   a. the newcomers made great efforts to create Jewish communities and preserve their traditions.
   b. there was a good deal of cooperation between Jews and Gentiles in many areas of life, including religion.
   c. the Ashkenazim and Sephardim argued over whose rituals and customs would be used in American synagogues.

Letters To The "Old Country"*

Jews who settled in the American colonies might have had families and friends in the "Old Country" to whom they would have written letters. The sentences below could have come from such letters. To which event does each refer?

1. We have been granted full religious freedom here in the name of the principle that all religions should be treated equally. And the man responsible for this is a clergyman.

2. You may ask: Why stir up a fuss over such a small thing? Because this "small thing" spells the difference between being first-class citizens and second-class citizens—between assuming responsibility for our own safety and security, and leaving our protection to other people.

3. This new state law is really a famous first. A person is guaranteed full rights regardless of religion. The American Revolution was more than just a political or military event; it was a revolution of ideas.

4. This document is a whole new chapter in our history. It gives us guarantees on a national scale. One day there might even be a Jewish president.

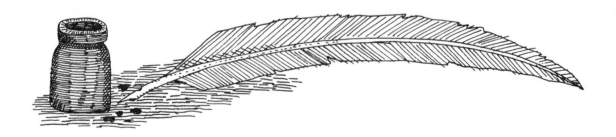

The Old And The New

There were great differences between the Jewish experience in Europe and the Jewish experience in North America. Think about them and then see if you can complete the following statements.

1. In Europe, Jews mostly lived in ghettos and shtetls; in the New World,

_____

_____

2. In Europe, Jews spoke their own language and generally lived a cultural life apart from the Christian majority; in the New World,

_____

_____

3. In the New World, Jews were full-fledged citizens with equal rights guaranteed by law; in Europe, for the most part,

_____

_____

4. In Europe, the church had a great deal of political power; in the New World,

_____

_____

5. In Europe, Jews were considered a minority of strangers and "guests" of the native population; in the New World,

_____

_____

In The News*

You have read about people who achieved important things for our country and for our people. These newspaper items could have been written about them. Can you identify the individual who is described in each?

1. He is a modern Moses, who dreams of gathering his people and leading them to a "Promised Land."

   _____

2. This man is determined to make waves. He fights against prejudice and serves his country heroically.

   _____

3. He is a Jewish plantation owner and secretary of war for the Confederacy. But how can a person, whose ancestors were slaves, serve a government that is dedicated to slavery?

   _____

4. He's a peddler with a tough product. His miner customers can give them a lot of wear and tear. His product will probably be around when the gold rush is just a page in the history books.

   _____

5. A war veteran and a successful businessman, but above all, this man is a committed member of the community, involved in most worthy causes.

   _____

An Occupation Scan*

Hidden in the letters below are ten occupations discussed in the chapter. Look across and down to find the hidden words.

```
S  A  I  L  O  R  G  M  T  M
H  P  W  T  R  A  D  E  R  E
E  M  L  E  D  B  W  B  X  R
R  I  E  A  C  B  R  A  Y  C
I  K  Y  B  N  I  I  N  F  H
F  O  T  A  N  T  T  K  K  A
F  Y  J  U  D  G  E  E  A  N
N  W  R  Z  X  Z  R  R  Q  T
P  O  L  I  T  I  C  I  A  N
P  E  D  D  L  E  R  G  D  B
```

_____   _____

_____   _____

_____   _____

_____   _____

How Do You Know?

Find a fact or quotation in the textbook to prove each statement.

1. Jews were involved not only with their own concerns, but with the larger community as well.

_____

_____

_____

2. Jews were experiencing trouble in other parts of the world.

_____

_____

_____

3. American Jews sometimes disagreed on important issues.

_____

_____

_____

4. America was a land of opportunity for Jews.

_____

_____

_____

5. American Jews were committed to helping one another.

_____

_____

_____

Frontier Family

The year is 1866, and you have just opened a general store in Dodge City. You are doing well financially. You get along with the local inhabitants, and you and your family plan to make this your permanent home. The only problem is that yours is the only Jewish family for 200 miles in any direction. You want to raise your children to be good Jews. What are some of the difficulties you are likely to encounter?

What are some of the steps you might take to overcome these difficulties?

_____

_____

_____

_____

_____

_____

_____

History Lessons

These are four important lessons we can learn from history. Select one and explain how you learned it and why it is important.

1. It is easier to change a law than to change people's feelings and attitudes.

2. An appeal to a government's "sense of justice" can be helped along by political and economic power.

3. One individual can make a great difference in how a particular event will turn out.

4. When the Jewish people unite, they can help one another in times of crisis.

_____

_____

_____

_____

_____

_____

_____

_____

_____

_____

_____

_____

_____

The Reasons Why

Complete each of the following statements.

1. It took nearly 100 years from the time of their emancipation in France for the Jews to win full rights of citizenship in Western Europe because

_____

_____

_____

2. Syria finally found the Jews accused of the Damascus Blood Libel innocent because

_____

_____

_____

3. Czarina Catherine II created the "Pale of Settlement" because

_____

_____

_____

4. The Alliance Israelite Universelle was established because

_____

_____

_____

5. Even though anti-Jewish laws were fast disappearing, anti-Jewish feelings were not because

_____

_____

_____

Events And Effects*

Match the event, in the left column, to the effect it produced, in the right column. Make your choice by placing the number of the event in the space next to its effect.

Event

1. The Damascus Blood Libel

2. The creation of the "Pale of Settlement"

3. The Kishinev Pogrom

4. The establishment of the Alliance Israelite Universelle

5. The assassination of Czar Alexander II

Effect

____ added strong and organized protection of the rights of Jews all over the world.

____ triggered a wave of pogroms throughout Russia, and paved the way for the "May Laws."

____ taught the Jews that they could unite and work together successfully on an international level.

____ made Polish Jewry "a nation within a nation," proving that a ghetto could be built on a nationwide scale.

____ made many Jews question their responses to anti-Semitic violence.

A Gallery Of Personalities*

Each of the personalities whose picture appears in the gallery below played an important role in the story of Jewish life in Europe during the past two centuries. On the basis of the description under the picture, write in the name of the personality.

A victim of blood libel accusations in Russia.

The English Jewish couple who helped to free the Jews accused of the Damascus Blood Libel.

The creator of the "Pale of Settlement."

A poet—the author of "The City of Slaughter."

A famous 19th century *shtadlan* who founded the Alliance Israelite Universelle.

The enemy of the Jews who brought the "May Laws" into being.

Who, What, And Where Am I?*

1. I am the place through which Eastern European Jews, and other immigrants, moved when they first arrived in America.

_____

2. I am the first Jew who served as a judge on the United States Supreme Court.

_____

3. Many immigrants worked within my four walls. I am small, dark, and stuffy, but I made a lot of money for my owners.

_____

4. I am a self-help organization set up according to a town or region in the "Old Country."

_____

5. We are the founders of the branch of Judaism known as Liberal and Reform.

_____

6. I am the movement that believes Jewish laws and rituals should stay as they are, but that the style of Jewish worship can be more modern. I also believe that science and religion need not be opposed to one another.

_____

7. I am the branch of Judaism that believes that when our tradition does change, it should do so very slowly, and should always be marked by a deep knowledge of, and respect for, the past. Today I am known as

_____

Causes And Consequences

Complete each of the following statements with one important consequence that it brought about.

1. Because the German Jews wanted to become as American as they could,

_____

_____

_____

2. Because there were more immigrants than there were jobs,

_____

_____

_____

3. Because Louis D. Brandeis believed so deeply in social justice,

_____

_____

_____

4. Because the Eastern European Jews understood that individual workers were helpless in dealing with their sweatshop bosses,

_____

_____

_____

5. Because of the rise of violent anti-Semitism in Eastern Europe after 1881,

_____

_____

_____

A Round-Table Discussion*

Four Jews are sitting around a table, having a heated discussion. The first is Orthodox, the second, New Orthodox, the third, Conservative, and the fourth, Reform. The statements below were made during the discussion. On the basis of what you know about these four approaches to Judaism, identify the speaker.

1. These are new and changing times, and there's nothing wrong with making our prayer services more modern. I think that organ music adds beauty to our services.

_____

2. Our heritage and tradition have kept us alive. Faith is our greatest strength. Science and religion have never mixed—and they never will.

_____

3. I am not against change, but is must happen slowly, and with thought and care. Judaism is thousands of years old—and there is much that we can learn from our past.

_____

4. Every law and every ceremony are sacred. Nothing should be changed. Nothing has to be changed. But being for tradition does not make me against beauty. And why shouldn't Jews study our teachings in a language that we understand?

_____

After Dinner Speeches*

A respected personality is often invited to speak publicly. Each of the following sentences could have been part of an introduction for one of the individuals you read about. Can you identify each person?

1. A courageous champion of the working man and a committed Zionist, who tried to create a school for rabbis of all movements. . .

---

2. A dedicated scholar, and a talented "treasure hunter". . .

---

3. Like our forefather Abraham, he left the land of his birth and traveled into a strange country. . . on behalf of his people. . .

---

4. A leader who dreamed of uniting all of American Jewry through prayer. . .

---

5. An educator who proved that a single institution could teach both traditional and secular subjects. . .

A Profile of American Judaism

You have read about the development of the three branches of Judaism in America. Fill in the scrolls with the missing information.

ORTHODOX

Leading Personalities

_____

_____

Rabbinical Training School(s)

_____

_____

Union of Synagogues

_____

_____

Additional Information

_____

_____

CONSERVATIVE

Leading Personalities

_____

_____

Rabbinical Training School(s)

_____

_____

Union of Synagogues

_____

_____

Additional Information

_____

_____

REFORM

Leading Personalities

_____

Rabbinical Training School(s)

_____

Union of Synagogues

_____

_____

Additional Information

_____

_____

Working Together

There are many shared areas of concern in Jewish life today. Orthodox, Conservative, and Reform Jews often work together to solve problems. Circle the number in front of each concern in which the three movements cooperate with one another.

1. Helping the Jewish poor.
2. Fighting anti-Semitism.
3. Working for Soviet Jewry.
4. Discouraging intermarriage.
5. Organizing a Jewish Book Month event.
6. Setting up a program of studies for religious school.
7. Participating in the United Jewish Appeal Campaign.
8. Revising the prayer book.
9. Establishing an Old Age Home.
10. Raising money for a Jewish hospital.

Historical Dictionary

Define each of the following terms.

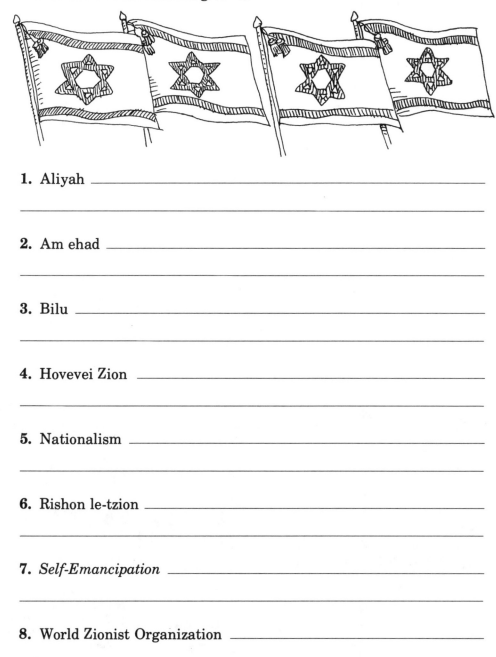

1. Aliyah _____

_____

2. Am ehad _____

_____

3. Bilu _____

_____

4. Hovevei Zion _____

_____

5. Nationalism _____

_____

6. Rishon le-tzion _____

_____

7. *Self-Emancipation* _____

_____

8. World Zionist Organization _____

_____

Effects

What were the most important effects of each of the following events?

1. The Dreyfus Trial

_____

_____

_____

2. The publication of *Self-Emancipation*

_____

_____

_____

3. The Zionist Congress

_____

_____

_____

4. The First Aliyah

_____

_____

_____

A Zionist Puzzle

The birth of Zionism can be compared to putting together a jigsaw puzzle. It developed from many different parts. Select one of the "pieces" and explain how it helped secure a permanent homeland for Jews everywhere.

STRONG LEADERSHIP

HEBREW LANGUAGE

SHARED HISTORY

ONE PEOPLE

NATIONALISM

LOVE OF THE LAND OF ISRAEL

YOUNG IDEALISTS

_____

_____

_____

_____

_____

_____

Your Interpretation

1. What does Herzl's saying, "If you will it, it is no dream," mean?

_____

_____

_____

2. When Dreyfus was dishonored, the cry of the crowd was, "Down with the Jews," not, "Down with the traitor." Why did this alarm Herzl?

_____

_____

_____

3. What are "arguments for the sake of heaven," and why are they considered good and healthy?

_____

_____

_____

4. Why is there such a powerful connection between the Jewish people and the land of Israel?

_____

_____

_____

5. In what ways are we _am ehad_—"One People"—today?

_____

_____

_____

Explanations

Write a brief explanation of each of the following terms.

1. Ha-Shomer

_____

_____

2. The Balfour Declaration

_____

_____

3. The "Religion of Labor"

_____

_____

4. The Second Aliyah

_____

_____

5. Kibbutz

_____

_____

6. Maskilim

_____

_____

7. Halutzim

_____

_____

The Reasons Why

1. Eliezer Ben-Yehuda believed in the rebirth of Hebrew as a living language because

_____

_____

2. The halutzim believed that it was important that they learn to use weapons and act as Shomerim because

_____

_____

3. Aaron David Gordon and his young friends from the Second Aliyah believed that Jewish settlers in Palestine should work as laborers on the land because

_____

_____

4. Many Orthodox Jews refused to speak everyday Hebrew because

_____

_____

5. The British issued the "Balfour Declaration" because

_____

_____

6. On the kibbutz, there are no rich people or poor people because

_____

_____

Going Up*

You have learned the word for immigration to Israel—*aliyah*. It means "going up." The scrambled ideas below represent steps up the Zionist ladder. Each step brought the Zionists closer to the realization of their dream. Unscramble each idea and write it in the step.

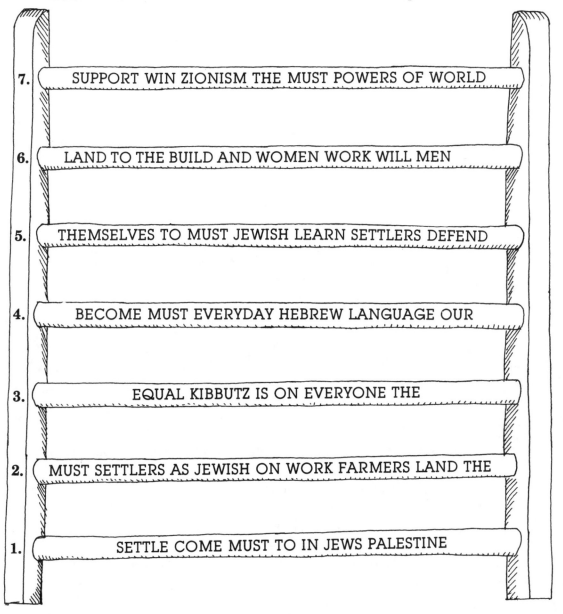

7. SUPPORT WIN ZIONISM THE MUST POWERS OF WORLD

6. LAND TO THE BUILD AND WOMEN WORK WILL MEN

5. THEMSELVES TO MUST JEWISH LEARN SETTLERS DEFEND

4. BECOME MUST EVERYDAY HEBREW LANGUAGE OUR

3. EQUAL KIBBUTZ IS ON EVERYONE THE

2. MUST SETTLERS AS JEWISH ON WORK FARMERS LAND THE

1. SETTLE COME MUST TO IN JEWS PALESTINE

A Pioneer's Tour

If young pioneers had taken a tour of Palestine, what would they have seen? Identify each of the "attractions." Write each number next to the matching name on the map.

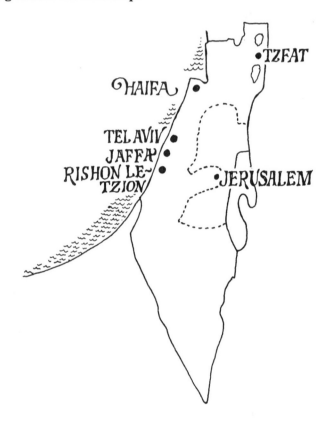

1. Israel's first kibbutz
2. An ancient port city, through which most of the early *halutzim* entered Palestine
3. Israel's ancient and modern capital
4. One of Israel's first Zionist settlements, built by the BILU
5. A port city—home of the Technion
6. The first all-Jewish city in modern times.
7. The beautiful old city of mystics, where Joseph Caro wrote the Shulhan Aruch.

A Review Of The Facts*

This chapter of the text tells of events that are almost impossible to imagine. Perhaps the best way to approach this material is to review the facts, and to ask ourselves a few basic questions—questions that may have no easy or certain answers.

1. The name of the book in which Hitler set down his racist ideas.

_____

2. Two Jewish leaders who refused to leave their people, even though it meant imprisonment (in one case) and death (in the other).

_____ and _____

3. The full name of the Nazi Party.

_____

4. The name of the Nazi emblem.

_____

5. The name of the program designed to murder every Jewish man, woman, and child in Europe.

_____

6. The death camp where more than two million Jews were murdered.

_____

7. Look at the map on page 127 of the text. In which country were the extermination camps located?

_____

8. The name given to non-Jews who, often at great risk, tried to save Jews (Hebrew and English).

_____ and _____

9. The place in Russia where more than 10,000 Jews were forced to dig their own graves, and were then shot and buried.

_____

Underground Diaries*

Some Jews tried to keep records of what was happening. Which event does each of these excerpts from imaginary diaries describe?

1. It is a moment of light in the middle of a nightmare. A handful of Jews, with practically no weapons at all, have held off the German army for nearly a month.

_____

2. They burned our synagogue. They broke the windows of my father's store and took away everything. They beat my brother when he tried to protest. And in the middle of the night, they came and arrested my father. The whole country has gone mad!

_____

3. Such a small country, and yet its people stood up to the Germans and rescued nearly every Jew in the country! Perhaps there is hope, after all. Perhaps we have not been abandoned altogether.

_____

Thoughts And Feelings

You have read about what many people call the worst crime in human history. It happened to your people—during the century in which you were born. What are your thoughts and feelings on the subject? What questions do you have? The space below is left blank for you to write or to draw in.

Words And Meanings*

Match the words in the left column with their proper meanings in the right column. Make your choice by placing the number of each word in the space next to its meaning.

1. Mellah

2. Sabra

3. Knesset

4. Yishuv

5. Aliyah Bet

6. Haganah

7. Mabarot (singular : Mabarah)

8. Youth Aliyah

—— The program of smuggling Jewish refugees into Palestine, in defiance of British policy

—— The temporary tent cities set up to house the huge flow of immigrants during the first years of statehood

—— A Jewish section, or ghetto

—— The secret defense force of the Jewish community in Palestine

—— Israel's National Assembly, or Parliament

—— An organization that rescued Jewish young people from Europe and helped them build new lives in Palestine

—— The popular nickname of native-born Israelis—taken from a cactus fruit which is prickly on the outside and sweet on the inside

—— The name of Palestine's Jewish population before the creation of the State of Israel

Problem Solving*

The history of the State of Israel can be read as a series of "problems-to-be-solved." The memos below could have come from the desks of Jewish officials.

MEMO #1

We will not accept the anti-immigration policy of the British government. Jewish refugees must have a home!

This problem was solved by

_____

_____

_____

MO

everyone. We must
ist, perhaps we can

The Arabs keep on att
nothing. We need our

MEMO #2

The Jews of the Yishuv need health care and proper medical facilities.

This problem was solved by

_____

_____

_____

MEMO #3

The Germans mean to kill everyone. We must do something! At the very least, perhaps we can save the children.

This problem was responded to by

_____

_____

_____

must have a home!

Biographical Dictionary

The following people were important to the State of Israel. Write what you have learned about each.

1. David Ben-Gurion

_____

_____

2. Rachel Yanait Ben-Zvi

_____

_____

3. Martin Buber

_____

_____

4. Abba Eban

_____

_____

5. Golda Meir

_____

_____

6. Henrietta Szold

_____

_____

7. Yigael Yadin

_____

_____

Causes and Consequences

Complete each of the following causes with at least one important consequence that it brought about.

1. Because the Arabs refused to accept the U.N. Partition Plan

_____

_____

_____

2. Because leaders like the Mufti of Jerusalem taught their followers that the Jews meant to drive all the Arabs out of Palestine

_____

_____

_____

3. Because the Arabs complained that too many Jews would come to Palestine

_____

_____

_____

4. Because some Jews refused to accept the presence of the British in Palestine

_____

_____

_____

5. Because the Arab nations never signed a peace treaty and never admitted Israel's right to exist,

_____

_____

_____

Events And Effects*

Match the event, in the left column, to its effect, in the right column.

Event

1. The discovery of the Dead Sea Scrolls

2. The Yom Kippur War

3. The Entebbe incident

4. The Treaty of Camp David

5. The flight of the Palestinians

6. The Six Day War

Effect

___ Set into motion a chain of developments that have troubled Israelis and Arabs since the creation of the State.

___ Made a break in the wall of non-communication which had separated Israelis and Arabs for 30 years.

___ Gave Israel stretches of territory that greatly improved its military and political position.

___ Showed Israelis how isolated they were in the world community.

___ Weakened the structure of international law by its example of an official government openly cooperating with terrorists.

___ Helped make archaeology Israel's "national sport," and Israelis aware of their historical roots in the land.

In the Headlines*

To which war or event does each of the following headlines refer?

1. **ISRAEL AND ALLIES VOW TO OPEN WATERWAY TO ALL NATIONS**

2. **JORDANIANS STAGE VICTORY CELEBRATION IN OLD JERUSALEM**

3. **PIECES OF BIBLE DISCOVERED AFTER 2000 YEARS**

4. **EUROPEAN ALLIES DENY LANDING RIGHTS TO AMERICAN PLANES AIRLIFTING ARMS TO ISRAEL**

5. **AFTER 19 YEARS, A UNITED JERUSALEM!**

6. **OFFICIALS ASSURE PUBLIC THAT THE GAMES WILL GO ON**

7. **THREE WORLD LEADERS JOIN HANDS TO WORK FOR PEACE**

8. **UPROAR IN U.N. OVER ISRAEL'S VIOLATION OF UGANDA'S RIGHTS**

Map Study*

Study the map on page 139, and then try to answer the following questions.

1. A person sunbathing on the beach of Eilat could look out at the territory of what two countries?

   _____ and _____

2. One of the constant Arab threats over the years was to push Israel into the sea. Which sea?

   _____

3. Any Arab country bordering on Israel is called a confrontation state. What are the confrontation states?

   _____, _____, _____, and _____

4. Before the Six Day War, one of the great dangers facing Israel was that the country could be cut in two by an invading Arab army. Which country's army could have done this easily?

   _____

5. In both the Suez and Six Day wars, Israel had to capture a port on the Sinai Peninsula to make sure that its ships could travel freely from Eilat to the Red Sea. What is the name of this port?

   _____

6. Before the Six Day War, Gaza was a staging area from which Palestinian terrorists raided Israeli villages. On the basis of what you see on the map, which Arab confrontation state trained and armed the terrorists?

   _____

Looking Inward

Many Israelis are looking inward and asking themselves questions about the meaning of their Jewish identity. You can try to do the same. Answer the following questions thoughtfully and honestly.

1. What do you like most about being Jewish?

_____

_____

_____

_____

2. Is there anything that bothers you about being Jewish?

_____

_____

_____

_____

3. What can you do, in practical terms, to lead a fuller and more satisfying Jewish life?

_____

_____

In Addition

Add one more fact or idea to each of the statements below. Make your addition on the basis of what you think is most important.

1. The Jews of Yemen
   a. lived in the country for more than 1,600 years.
   b. experienced persecution from time to time.
In addition,

_____

2. The Falashas
   a. have lived in what is now Ethiopia since the time of the First Temple.
   b. are victims of poverty, disease, starvation, and government oppression today.
In addition,

_____

3. Soviet Union Jews
   a. make up the third largest Jewish community in the world today.
   b. face many cruel obstacles when they try to live as Jews.
In addition,

_____

4. The Jews in Arab lands
   a. are often hated by their non-Jewish neighbors.
   b. In addition,

_____

5. Jews in the lands of freedom
   a. are fully accepted as equal citizens.
   b. are not made to feel separate from their non-Jewish neighbors.
In addition,

_____

History Lessons

Each of these lessons of history is found in your textbook. Choose one and explain why the lesson is important.

1. Israel is made up of Jews from many different countries and cultures.

2. Freedom presents its own set of dangers to Jewish survival.

3. There are some Jewish communities that have been cut off from other Jews for hundreds or even thousands of years.

4. The idea that "every Jew is responsible for every other Jew" has been put into practice often in recent years.

_____

_____

_____

_____

_____

_____

_____

_____

_____

Identity Builders

Imagine that you are on a trip to the Soviet Union. There you have met and made friends with a Jewish family from Kiev. They tell you that they have just received some Jewish books which were smuggled in for them. They intend to begin studying at once. They ask you how each of the following subjects helps build Jewish identity. How would you explain?

1. Jewish History

_____

_____

2. The Hebrew Language

_____

_____

3. The Holocaust

_____

_____

4. The Bible

_____

_____

5. Jewish Holidays

_____

_____

6. The State of Israel

_____

_____

True Or False*

1. Next to Israel, the United States has the largest Jewish population in the world. ( )

2. Fewer Jews speak Yiddish today than they did thirty years ago. ( )

3. Jews are free to enter almost every professional field in the United States. ( )

4. American Jews have never experienced anti-Semitism. ( )

5. Women serve as rabbis and cantors in the Reform and Reconstructionist movements. ( )

6. One of the values of the *Havurah* is a strong, closely-knit Jewish community. ( )

7. The Hasidim refuse to have anything to do with Jews who have not adopted their lifestyle and religious approach. ( )

8. Reconstructionism believes that the true center of Judaism is the Jewish people. ( )

9. There are fewer Jewish schools in the United States today than there were thirty years ago. ( )

10. The Jewish tzedakah network reaches out to Jews all over the world. ( )

Explanations

Explain the following statements.

1. The tradition of freedom in this country helped shape the course of American Jewish history.

_____

_____

_____

2. The Holocaust has influenced American Jewish thinking.

_____

_____

_____

3. American Jews have been successful in almost every walk of life.

_____

_____

_____

4. The tzedakah network is called one of the greatest contributions of American Jewry.

_____

_____

_____

The Traveling Dollar

Some claim that "money talks"—and this dollar has a lot to say. It has traveled through the Jewish tzedakah network. What did it do, along with many other dollars, and whom did it help? Explain how funds are used in the following areas:

1. Education

_____

_____

_____

2. Community Services

_____

_____

_____

3. Israel

_____

_____

_____

4. Jewish Communities in other countries

_____

_____

_____

Idea Scramble*

Unscramble each of the word groups below to discover the ideas that
have been important in American Jewish life.

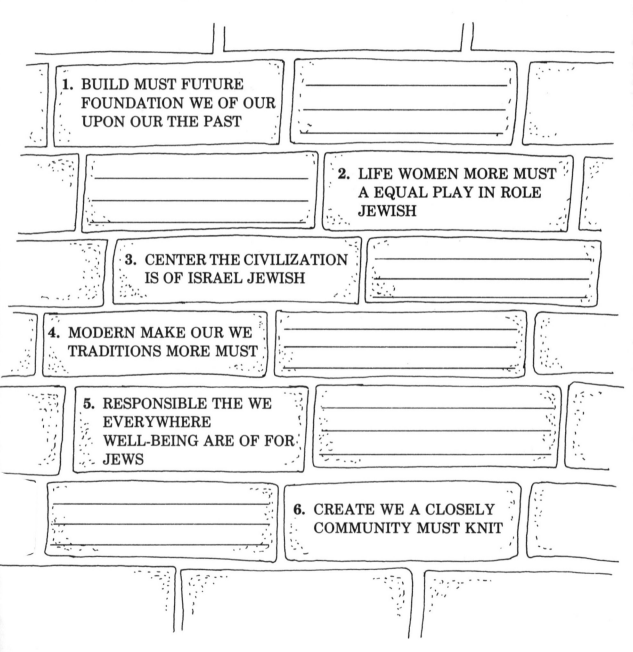

1. BUILD MUST FUTURE FOUNDATION WE OF OUR UPON OUR THE PAST

2. LIFE WOMEN MORE MUST A EQUAL PLAY IN ROLE JEWISH

3. CENTER THE CIVILIZATION IS OF ISRAEL JEWISH

4. MODERN MAKE OUR WE TRADITIONS MORE MUST

5. RESPONSIBLE THE WE EVERYWHERE WELL-BEING ARE OF FOR JEWS

6. CREATE WE A CLOSELY COMMUNITY MUST KNIT

Places We Have Visited*

1. The Syrian city associated with a notorious blood libel

---

2. The Russian city in which a vicious pogrom took place, which moved Bialik to write CITY OF SLAUGHTER

---

3. The ancient and modern capital of Israel

---

4. The first all-Jewish city in modern Israel

---

5. The place where the most famous act of Jewish resistance of World War II occurred—a handful of Jewish fighters held off the Germans for nearly a month

---

6. The North American city, in which the first Jewish immigrants arrived and settled back in 1654

---

7. The place where the Israeli-Egyptian peace treaty was signed

---

8. The extermination camp in Poland where more than two million Jews were murdered

---

9. The country from where the Falashas come

---

10. The area in Russia and Poland to which most Eastern European Jews were confined

---

Events We Have Witnessed*

1. It convinced Herzl of the need for Zionism

2. The worst crime in human history, in which six million Jews were murdered

3. England's official promise to help create a Jewish homeland

4. The end of 2,000 years of Jewish statelessness

5. The war that brought about a united Jerusalem

6. It marked the first time since the days of the Romans that the Jews were made equal under the law

7. The efforts to capture Palestine for Christianity which resulted in the murder of thousands of Jews

8. It helped make archaeology Israel's national "sport"

People We Have Met*

1. The French Jewish scholar who wrote commentaries on nearly all the books of the Bible and Talmud

___

2. The author of the Shulhan Aruch

___

3. The greatest of all Spanish Jews, author of MISHNEH TORAH and THE GUIDE TO THE PERPLEXED

___

4. The "Angel of the Marranos" who brought many persecuted Jews to settle in Turkey

___

5. The Dutch Jew who persuaded Cromwell to allow the Jews—who had been expelled 300 years earlier—to return to England

___

6. The most important teacher of mysticism and of the Zohar, his teachings spread throughout the Jewish world

___

7. The founder of the Hasidic movement

___

8. The German Jew, known as the "father of the Haskalah"

___

9. The man who began the "Science of Judaism"

___

10. The Hebrew poet who wrote "The City Of Slaughter"

___

More People We Have Met*

11. The father of modern Zionism, and author of THE JEWISH STATE

12. The pioneers who came to Israel on the First Aliyah

13. The man who wrote of a "religion of labor," and who settled on Kibbutz Deganyah at the age of 48

14. The man who was mainly responsible for the revival of Hebrew as a living language

15. The woman who founded Hadassah and Youth Aliyah

16. Israel's first prime minister

17. Israel's first president

18. The German-born Jew, generally considered the greatest scientist of modern times, who discovered the Law of Relativity

19. The woman who became Israel's prime minister

20. The first—and so far, only—Arab leader to sign a peace treaty with Israel

Highlights Of Our Journey

Which part of our journey through Jewish history interested you the most and why?

_____

_____

_____

What were the most important lessons that you learned from:
The history of the Spanish Jewish community?

_____

_____

_____

The history of the American Jewish community?

_____

_____

_____

The Holocaust?

_____

_____

_____

The rebirth of the State of Israel?

_____

_____

_____

To Our Continuing Journey — Shalom!

START→

Answer Key*

This activity book has two kinds of questions: those that may be answered by referring to specific facts in the textbook; and those that require the students to interpret the material being studied in the light of their own ideas. The following key provides answers *only* for questions that are factual in nature.

  5 *Who Were They?* 3; 8; 1; 2; 7; 4; 5; 9; 6

  7 *Secrets Of Survival* TORAH; TALMUD; PRAYER; FAITH; STUDY; COVENANT; COMMUNITY

  8 *Who, What, And Where Am I?* 1. ROME 2. CONSTANTINE 3. POPE GREGORY 4. ASHKENAZ 5. RASHI 6. A CRUSADER 7. KIDDUSH HA-SHEM 8. RABBI YOM TOV BEN ISAAC OF YORK

 12 *Read All About It!* 1. THE BLOOD LIBEL IN NORWICH, ENGLAND
    2. THE BURNING OF TALMUDS IN FRONT OF NOTRE DAME CATHEDRAL
    3. RABBI MEIR OF ROTTENBERG'S REFUSAL TO BE RANSOMED 4. THE JEWS WERE ACCUSED OF POISONING THE WELLS, AND SO CAUSING THE BLACK DEATH 5. POPE INNOCENT'S ORDER THAT THE JEWS WEAR SPECIAL CLOTHING
    6. NAHMANIDES' EXPULSION FROM SPAIN AFTER WINNING THE DISPUTATION

 14 *Words And Meanings* 4; 6; 5; 3; 1; 2

 17 *Who, What, And Where Am I?* 1. VA'AD ARBA ARATZOT (THE COUNCIL OF THE FOUR LANDS) 2. PRINTING PRESS 3. GHETTO
    4. SHULHAN ARUCH 5. JOSEPH CARO 6. SHTETL 7. TZEDAKAH 8. AZARIAH DEI ROSSI 9. MOSES ISSERLES

 21 *The Five Pillars Of Islam* 1. THERE IS BUT ONE GOD AND HIS NAME IS ALLAH 2. A MUSLIM MUST PRAY TO GOD EVERY SINGLE DAY
    3. FASTING IS A WAY OF PRAYING TO GOD 4. LEND A HELPING HAND TO THE POOR PEOPLE IN YOUR MIDST 5. MAKE A PILGRIMAGE TO THE HOLY PLACES OF ISLAM

 22 *A Merchant's Journal* 1. MECCA 2. THE RED SEA 3. YATHRIB (LATER CALLED MEDINA) 4. THE DOME OF THE ROCK, OR THE MOSQUE OF OMAR
    5. DAMASCUS 6. JERUSALEM

 24 *Notable Achievements* 1. JUDAH HALEVI 2. SAMUEL HA-NAGID (SAMUEL "THE PRINCE") 3. HISDAI IBN SHAPRUT 4. MOSES IBN EZRA
    5. MAIMONIDES 6. SOLOMON IBN GABIROL

 25 *Book Reviews* 1. *THE GUIDE TO THE PERPLEXED* BY MAIMONIDES
    2. *SEFER HA KUZARI* ("THE BOOK OF THE KHAZARS") BY JUDAH HALEVI
    3. *THE SIDDUR* BY RAV AMRAM 4. *THE DUTIES OF THE HEART* BY BAHYA IBN PAQUADA 5. *MISHNEH TORAH* BY MAIMONIDES

 28 *Who, What, When, And Where Am I?* 1. 1492 2. RECIFE, BRAZIL
    3. GRANADA 4. MARRANO 5. NEW AMSTERDAM (LATER KNOWN AS NEW YORK)
    6. CONQUISTADORES 7. TOMAS DE TORQUEMADA

 29 *The Ingredients Of The Inquisition* 4

 30 *On The Move* 1. LISBON, PORTUGAL 2. ALEXANDRIA, EGYPT
    3. LONDON, ENGLAND 4. ROME, ITALY 5. CONSTANTINOPLE, TURKEY
    6. AMSTERDAM, HOLLAND

96 Notes